A P E

MW01241846

PERSONAL PRAYERS
IN
TIMES OF ILLNESS

HENRY PALENSCHUS

DIMENSIONS
FOR LIVING
NASHVILLE

PERSONAL PRAYERS IN TIMES OF ILLNESS

02 03 04 05 06 07 08 09 10 11—10 9 8 7 6 5 4 3 2 1

MANUFACTURED IN THE UNITED STATES OF AMERICA

Resting

Lord Jesus, I know how important it is for me to rest if I am to get well; yet I find it so hard to rest. I can't switch off.

I constantly find myself thinking about the things that need doing. In my mind I am still controlling, guiding, checking, and worrying how things will go without me. Lord, help me to switch off. Help me, Lord of my life, to put everything in your good and loving hands, for you to control, guide, and check.

And so let me rest.

And when my mind races, let your word of promise quiet me.

"Be still, and know that I am God" (Psalm 46:10).
Be still . . . I am God. . . .
Be still . . . I am God. . . . Amen.

FEAR

Lord Jesus, I am gripped by fear, and it's a grip from which I can't break free. I try to fight it, but nothing seems effective against it.

I see clearly how fear feeds off itself; I find myself thinking the worst, rather than the best.

I recognize that the real sting, the real thorn in my side, is not just my illness but fear of the outcome.

I know too that the answer to my fear is a radical trust in you. Grant me such trust. Help me to trust too that you have a way for me. Keep me hopeful. Amen.

BEFORE AN OPERATION

I know that soon they will be wheeling me into the operating room. Lord Jesus, you know how fearful I am about this. I just wish it would hurry up and happen; this waiting is awful.

What I fear is the loss of consciousness. I fear the blackness. I fear that the outcome of the operation may be unsatisfactory, or that there will be complications.

Go with me into this operation. Let me sense your presence now and as I go under. Hold me in the blackness. Be there with your presence as I awake. How comforting to me now are the words of the psalmist:

"Where can I go from your Spirit?
    Where can I flee from your presence?
If I go up to the heavens, you are there;
    if I make my bed in the depths, you are there. . . .
Your right hand will hold me fast."

(Psalm 139:7, 8, 10)

Amen.

In vain

Lord Jesus, I saw my aged neighbor raking the leaves off his front yard. This is quite an effort for him now, and the task left him exhausted. Then the wind returned, and his efforts were all in vain.

Lord, you know the efforts I have made with my illness. You know I have struggled, and at times how tired it has left me. Let it not be all in vain.

Let me continue to seek your face. Let me know something of the transforming power of your grace in my illness.

Purify and strengthen my faith so that my illness may not have been in vain, and then when it's over may there be some permanent gains.

And should the leaves of indifference and lukewarmness in faith and love return, let me, strengthened by this experience, be enabled to sweep them away yet again. Amen.

SLEEPLESSNESS

Lord Jesus, you know how poorly I have been sleeping lately. You know how tired I have been when I go to work the following day.

Lord, you know too the cause of my sleeplessness.

When I awake in the early hours, my problems seem magnified in the silence. Like mountains they loom before me.

Lord Jesus, I remember your word that faith can remove mountains. Grant me such a faith. Let me trust that you can remove the obstacles that lie before me, that you may pave a way for me. Free me from the foolish notion that it all depends on me. Free me from the foolish notion that unless I can continue to hold up the various structures of my life—my family, work, business, church committees, friends—then everything will collapse. Just enable me to let go, and grant me rest and peace.

Grant me a faith that can move mountains like that, Lord. Amen.

Discouragement

Lord Jesus, when I drive through thick fog, how slowly and deliberately I have to proceed. How tense I become from having to concentrate more. How monotonous it becomes after a while when I can't see the countryside, how claustrophobic.

A spiritual fog of discouragement has settled on me. It limits my vision, produces tensions, and causes me to see everything in shades of gray instead of their proper colors and variety. Worse still, Lord, I notice that I am enveloping my friends in the same fog, and you know how I value them and their encouragement.

But I am aware too that I must own my life again. Help me encourage myself in the same way that "David found strength in the LORD his God" (1 Samuel 30:6). Enable me to go over my life, prayerfully remembering with thankfulness your goodness and love shown to me in the past, and so let me gain confidence and encouragement for my continuing life with you. Help me dispel this fog of discouragement. Amen.

RESISTANCE TO GOD

Lord, I can't pray. I just do not have the inclination, and when I do try to pray I have no sense of your presence. There is an inner resistance to my customary contact with you.

Help me explore the meaning of this resistance and overcome it.

Is it an unexpressed anger at you that you might have caused this illness? If so, then like the psalmists of old enable me to express it. Is it my fear? Then help me to overcome it.

Is it my unbelief in your power to help? Then help my unbelief. Is it my current physical weakness? Then grant me patience to wait for it to improve. Lord, in you is life.

Restore your life in me, and strengthen and restore the life in my ailing body. Amen.

SOUNDS IN THE NIGHT

Once again I have awoken in the early morning.

It's become a regular thing, Lord. At first it used to upset me, and I fought it, but now I just listen to the sounds.

I listen to the quiet comings and goings, the workings of a hospital at night. I hear the subdued laughter of a nurse in the nurses' station. I hear the clink of medicine bottles on a cart, a muffled cough, footsteps—sounds of a caring institution.

And from the silence within I become mindful of your caring presence within me as I hear you say: "He who watches over you will not slumber" (Psalm 121:3).

And I respond quietly with the psalmist: "When I awake, I am still with you" (Psalm 139:18). Amen.

THE MUSTARD SEED

Lord Jesus, fancy someone giving me a gift of a pot of earth with a mustard seed in it! How I wish it would sprout and I could see the first shoot pressing through the earth.

It's teaching me patience—patience with myself and the course of my illness.

I wonder what's happening to the seed in the blackness of the earth? It's breaking up, Lord, coming apart, that's what is happening. But in the process a shoot is developing, pressing upward through the blackness to the day. It's like my faith and hope, springing up from the darkness, reaching up toward the day.

Thank you, Lord, for this symbol of hope—a symbol of your power in me, and the kingdom within. Amen.

ANGELS

Lord Jesus, I saw the face of fear today. I saw it in a woman who knew she was going to die. I know too that you understand her fear.

You yourself once prayed: "Father, if you are willing, take this cup from me." Lord, angels came and ministered to you in your agony, strengthening you.

I saw people go to this woman. The nurses adjusted her bedding and saw to her comforts, showing a great deal of kindness. The doctor did what he could with medicines and drugs. Friends put aside their fears, bringing their love and compassion. These people were angels ministering to her, strengthening her.

I thank you, Lord, for the angels you have sent to me. Amen.

MAKING NEW

Lord Jesus, you make all things new.

Wherever you went, you brought new life—life to the sick, to those whose minds were darkened, to hearts hardened by sin.

But you never *commanded* newness. You gave no recipe, no five easy steps. You *make* new, that's what's so amazing.

Through the agony of your cross you are able to enter into our deepest darkness and brokenness. Here the love that shines from your cross can heal and transform and rebuild.

Thank you for the transforming power of your cross. Thank you that through it you can rebuild and make all things new. Amen.

A WORD FOR THE WEARY

Lord Jesus, I thank you that "morning by morning [you waken] my ear to listen like one being taught" (Isaiah 50:4). You know how much I am in need of your teaching. You know how weary my illness has left me.

I am tired of the treatments, tired of the isolation, tired of the lack of meaningful activity, tired of fighting anxiety and depression. How welcome, then, is this news that you particularly want to teach me with a "word that sustains the weary."

Lord, as I reflect on your life I recognize this as central to what you taught and did. Help me be open to your teaching. Help me turn to it first thing each morning.

And as I prayerfully reflect on your promises, strengthen my resolve to fight on, as your prophet did when he said: "I have not been rebellious. . . . I set my face like flint. . . . I will not be put to shame" (Isaiah 50:5, 7). Amen.

WAITING

It's Advent, Lord. The church is in the waiting mode—waiting for you to come.

I am waiting too, waiting for your help and healing.

It's good to be able to look away from self, and look to you. I've noticed, Lord, how waiting is not a passive state, but an active thing. It requires me to look away from myself, not in self-negation, but in the belief that my true self, my healed self, lies ahead of me and has to do with your coming.

We are shaped, Lord, by what we love and what we long for. We bring a little of what we await into the present. Thank you that in my waiting I can know something of your presence now, and something of your help and healing now. "My soul waits for the Lord" (Psalm 130:6). Amen.

THE TRY

It was a World Cup rugby match, and my team was playing. I'm not normally interested in rugby, Lord, but I couldn't resist watching. What a magic moment when we scored the winning try! The replay in slow motion said it all, as the winger artfully threaded his way through the gaps in the defense, putting the ball over the line.

The whole stadium erupted. It was a moment of pure joy for the team and supporters. Lord, that's how I feel right now. I feel as if I have scored a try. For the first time I am confident I am on the mend, and that the improvement in my symptoms is not temporary.

It's a great moment, Lord. I throw my praise up to you, as I inwardly jubilantly punch the air. Amen.

Seedtime and harvest

Lord, all she could talk about was when she would be going home. She saw her illness merely as a temporary aberration that would soon be over. There was so much denial there, Lord. She seemed quite unable to understand or accept the situation she was in.

I became aware of how people see less and less meaning in suffering. Yet in spite of all our legitimate efforts to avoid it, suffering is a part of our lives, and quite often it can be a seed from which a harvest can come.

Lord, help me to learn to sow, expecting a harvest.

Help me not to deny suffering, but to see in it your appointed order of seedtime and harvest. Let me know the joy of the harvest as the psalmist did when he said: "He who goes out weeping, carrying seed to sow, will return with songs of joy, carrying sheaves with him" (Psalm 126:6). Amen.

MY TRUE SELF

Lord, I feel like a house whose supports are crumbling.

I have had to stop working. I have had to adjust my material lifestyle. My friends come less frequently. I can no longer enjoy the same experiences I enjoyed before. What's left when all these supports of my ego are taken away?

What's left, Lord Jesus, is you. My true self is left. What's lost is my "illusionary" self, or my "shadow" self as Thomas Merton called it. What's lost is the facade behind which I have been able to hide from you.

How strange my true self feels to me. It feels like dying. Is there no easier way to enter the Kingdom, Lord? Is there not an easier way to find my true self? Amen.

SOMETHING TO SAY

Lord, people often have nothing to say to each other. But I thank you for your word and your gospel. You always have something to say, something that uplifts, sustains, heals.

I thank you for the power of your word that can speak into situations that leave us with absolutely nothing to say. I thank you for the people who have been able to say something to me, and I thank you that I can share your word with others.

I thank you for these words from St. Paul: "Now we know that if the earthly tent we live in is destroyed, we have a building from God, an eternal house in heaven, not built by human hands. Meanwhile we groan, longing to be clothed with our heavenly dwelling. . . . Now it is God who has made us for this very purpose and has given us the Spirit as a deposit, guaranteeing what is to come" (2 Corinthians 5:1, 2, 5). Amen.

A SCRATCHED RECORD

Lord, my life has become like a scratchy record. There is so much background noise that the melody is barely audible.

I have become aware of the background stress in my life: stress that I have simply ignored and refused to recognize; stresses that come from difficulties in my work; stresses in my relationships at home, which I have ignored for fear of opening a Pandora's box; stresses that come from the way I see myself. I know these stresses have contributed to my illness.

Lord Jesus, I don't just want to get well again, I want to be whole. Heal me, Lord, and help me to deal with the background stresses of my life. Don't let the noise drown out the melody of my life.

"Heal me, O Lord, and I will be healed; save me and I will be saved, for you are the one I praise" (Jeremiah 17:14). Amen.

FOR THE SKILL OF THE SURGEON

Thank you, Lord, for the skill and knowledge of the surgeons. Thank you that I could entrust myself to them, and that the trust was not misplaced.

Bless the doctors and nurses who do this responsible and stressful work.

Ultimately, Lord, all healing comes from you. The skill of the surgeon would be wasted without the innate capacity of the body to heal itself. But it is part of your divine plan that we should be dependent on one another.

Lord, I am thankful for what the surgeon did. He didn't just attend to a diseased organ, but he was your instrument in my healing. Bless him according to your word: "He who refreshes others will himself be refreshed" (Proverbs 11:25). Amen.

SACRAMENT OF THE PRESENT MOMENT

Lord Jesus, I am watching a bird building a nest outside my window. I am captivated by this glimpse of vibrant life. "A sacrament of the present moment" someone called an experience like this, and so it is.

Lord, you watched the birds, the lilies, the fig tree, a mother hen and her chickens—ordinary things that spoke to you of the Kingdom.

Thank you for your life all around me, your life in a gift of flowers, in the laughter of a friend, in the unabashed spontaneity of a child—"sacraments of the present moment," through which you uplift, sustain, and inspire me to get well so that I can participate fully in life again. Amen.

ALL SHALL BE WELL

I have always loved those words of Lady Julian of Norwich: "All shall be well and all shall be well and all manner of things shall be well."

She lived a hard life, Lord, yet her life breathes a quiet warmth and confidence that is born of trust in you and your love. This attitude of joyful trust has been an inspiration to me. I so easily lose confidence when I am confronted by some bad news, or when the course of my illness takes a temporary step backwards, or when I develop a new, hitherto unexplained symptom.

Thank you, Lord, for all those people who have in some way reassured me that "all shall be well," who have in some way communicated to me the message: "Here, take some of my strength." I believe I am learning this joyful, confident trust, learning to say: "All shall be well . . . and all manner of things shall be well." Amen.

SEE AND PERCEIVE

Lord, you said it was possible to see but not perceive, to hear but not understand. I am aware that few people see the pain behind the smile or perceive the anxiety behind a pleasant exterior.

Some do, Lord. I thank you for those people and the healing they bring. I guess it could be said that I am well cared for here. But it's not the care of being accepted in my suffering. It's not the care of being taken out of my isolation.

I know, Lord, that you see and perceive, you hear and understand. Thank you for your loving acceptance of me in my brokenness. Let me see your loving purposes for my life. Enable me to perceive your gracious will for me. Amen.

A TRUE FRIEND

Lord Jesus, you know how thankful I am for the many people who have come to see me. But I am particularly thankful for that friend who truly listened to me.

In some societies illness is seen as the loss of one's soul. The task of the healer is to enter the spirit realm to find and bring back the lost soul.

I thank you for my friend who traveled with me through the landscape of my soul; who entered into the realm of my spirit, with its ups and particularly its downs. In so doing, this friend helped restore my soul, gave me hope, and aided my healing—at some cost to my friend.

I thank you especially, Lord, that you are my friend and brother, that you have shared this time with me. I thank you that with the psalmist I can say of you: "He restores my soul" (Psalm 23:3). Amen.

My shadow

Lord Jesus, my illness has stripped me of illusions about myself. I am aware that I am not as courageous or independent as I believed. In fact, I feel fearful and insecure. I need others, I need their strength.

There is another side to me that I wasn't aware of, a shadow side. I can't run away from my shadow, but I can find refuge in the shadow of your cross, Lord.

I thank you for the unconditional love and mercy that I find there, which enables me to accept my shadow. Having accepted more of myself, I feel more at peace. I feel stronger to face the time ahead. I thank you for your cross and the power of your love that comes from it. Amen.

A MOUNTAIN CLIMBER

Lord, I watched a mountain climber on TV. He climbed a sheer rock face. At first glance, it seemed impossible—but the mountain climber tackled his obstacle one step at a time. The steps were measured, not rushed. He never took two steps at once, nor were the steps too big. Each step taken gave confidence for the next one. A rushed climb would lead to exhaustion, and the climb would have to be abandoned.

Lord, help me to learn from the mountain climber. One step at a time is all that I need to take, each step appropriate to my strength and circumstance.

Lord, give me the confidence to tackle my illness in that way. Give me the confidence of the psalmist who said: "He will keep me safe . . . and set me high upon a rock" (Psalm 27:5). Amen.

Speak the Word

Lord, even in human terms, a word can be a powerful thing. It can send men into battle. It can reconcile two estranged people. A word of forgiveness can remove a mountain of guilt. A word of encouragement can cause a person to double his, or her efforts.

If a human word can do all that, your word can do so much more. The Roman centurion knew that when he said: "Just say the word, and my servant will be healed" (Matthew 8:8).

Lord, speak your healing word to me, and let me hear it. Speak the word I need, and grant what you speak. If it is *persevere*, then give me the strength I need. If it is *courage*, restore my spirit. If it is a loving word, let it penetrate my fears. Just say the word, Lord, and I will be healed. Amen.

THANKFULNESS

Lord Jesus, when I became aware of symptoms of illness in my body, I became concerned. The probing questions of the doctor added to my anxiety.

Then there were the X-rays and examinations, and the waiting for the results of the tests. Finally, I felt devastated when it was discovered that there was indeed a problem. And then came the amazing news that the illness was only in its infancy and would be completely cured.

Lord, I felt as if I was born again, that my life was given back to me as a gift for which I was enormously thankful.

Lord, why can't it be like that all the time? Why must I experience something like this before I learn to give thanks for my life and your many blessings to me? I just want to say with the psalmist: "Praise the LORD, O my soul, and forget not all his benefits" (Psalm 103:2). Amen.

THE WELL

Lord, wells in the desert have always been precious. A good well can make a desert area bloom. But neglected, these sources become swampy, polluted, unable to support life in the wilderness.

Lord, I have neglected the well within me. My illness has made me aware how dry it is. I want to restore the sources that have become silted and blocked. Help me to free them again.

Lord Jesus, you said: "Whoever drinks the water I give him will never thirst. Indeed, the water I give him will become in him a spring of water welling up to eternal life" (John 4:14).

Your life "welling up" in me, that's what I need. Help me to uncover this source of hope and healing again. Amen.

TIMES AND SEASONS

Lord, you want us to live ordered, not chaotic, lives. There is to be a time and a season for everything, a rhythm. Just as night follows day, periods of rest must follow periods of work.

I have ignored this rhythm. I have given my body and mind little rest, so now it has forced rest upon me. I am sick. I have pushed my body and my mind not only in special circumstances but as a matter of habit. I have not allowed sufficient time for recreation and rest.

I know too, Lord, that I will accomplish order and rhythm on the outside only if there is order and rhythm on the inside, so I pray with the hymnwriter:

"Take from our souls the strains and stress,
and let our ordered lives confess
the beauty of thy peace." Amen.

Joy in God's guidance

Lord, my mental horizons have narrowed since my illness. I feel hemmed in, confined, overwhelmed.

The psalmist praises you as a God who leads him out into a spacious place, "a place of abundance" (Psalm 66:12). He rejoices in your guidance through ordeals of "fire and water." He praises you for his liberation from a bird-catcher's snare, to know again the freedom of the open skies (Psalm 124:7).

Let me find joy in the knowledge of your guidance. Let me praise you.

I notice that the very act of praising you leads me into the spacious place the psalmist talks about.

I thank you, Lord, that you lead my soul into that spacious place.

Continue to lead me. How different things appear from here! Amen.

I WILL

Lord Jesus, since my illness I have often become passive and withdrawn. I know this is not good, because it aggravates my feelings of helplessness and leads me to believe my condition is worse than it really is.

Somehow I have convinced myself that I can't do certain things, when in fact I can. When I say I can't, as I often do, what I really mean is I won't.

Help me say I will, and follow through with it.

I will write that letter.
I will seek out company and not avoid it.
I will structure my day.
I will think of some little ways I can reward myself for tasks accomplished.

I will repeat to myself quietly and often: "I can do everything through him who gives me strength" (Philippians 4:13). Amen.

HEALING SILENCE

Lord, I love the quiet of this place. The twittering of the birds under the eaves magnifies the silence. This is a privileged place, because it helps me to attend to you better.

Here in this church, your presence is more real to me. Here the silence is filled with your presence.

I thank you that my body is the temple of the Holy Spirit. But it's a temple in a state of disrepair and some ruin, as you know, Lord. My illness fills the silence within me with discord and pain, rather than your joyful presence.

Restore your temple. Let me know again the joy of your silence, the joy of your loving presence. Let the silence of this place do its healing work within me. Amen.

Nagging pain

Lord, I know it's not a serious illness, just a low-level nagging pain. But it is a constant irritation and gets me down. It makes me less effective in my work, and I'm sure people notice my irritability.

I know I cannot always take something for the pain. I know, too, that in the long run it's better to put up with a certain measure of pain than risk the complications that could arise from constant medication. Help me, Lord, to go about my life in a more relaxed way, and so minimize my drug intake.

I'm inspired by St. Paul who spoke of "a thorn in my flesh." He had no recourse to drug remedies, yet he worked effectively and mightily in the church of God. You gave him the faith to accept your answer: "My grace is sufficient for you" (2 Corinthians 12:9).

Lord, either take away this pain or give me that grace which is "sufficient." Show your power in my weakness. Amen.

CLOSE TO DESPAIR

Lord, I have been in pain for weeks, and I admit I am close to despair. I find I am asking the age-old question: Why, Lord? And because there is no good answer, I begin to doubt your goodness. Why don't you help? If you are there, why don't you do something? The temptation to lose trust in your goodness can be strong at times.

Lord Jesus, I know you weren't spared this temptation either, but you overcame it through constant prayer. Prayer was as natural to you as breathing. Only prayer exercised in good times enabled you to see God's guiding hand in bad times.

Lord, that's how you overcame the temptation to despair in the Garden of Gethsemane; that's the only way it can be overcome. Help me to overcome. Help me to be hopeful again. Help me to heed your word to watch and pray, lest I despair. Amen.

Not hungry

Lord Jesus, my friends and relatives are concerned about me because I am not eating regularly. I just do not feel like it. Food is farthest from my mind at present. But I know I must eat, and I am prepared to take a little soup.

Lord, I also haven't been praying or reading your word much lately, either. Once again, I just do not feel like it. When I am well, I am inspired by the positive, dynamic images of the Kingdom: life as a wedding celebration, as a dance, as discovery and growth. These images and others rarely fail to uplift, and to bring joy and give direction. But I just do not feel like them at present.

Still, that's no excuse for not reading your word at all. It's no excuse for not praying. Here too I know that while I may not feel disciplined to eat meat, I do need at least to take a little "soup." Amen.

THE WORK OF SUFFERING

Lord, I never thought that I would miss my work, but I do now. I miss my colleagues. I miss feeling useful. I feel so frustrated and disappointed. I know I am going to have to work through these feelings if I am going to get better.

Help me, Lord, to do this work, and help me to accept that this is my true work at the present time, and that although it is difficult it is useful work.

I bring to you my frustration and disappointment, and as I work through them let me see the result of my work as you promised in Isaiah 53: "After the suffering of his soul, he will see the light of life and be satisfied" (v. 11). Amen.

THE GOLF CLUBS

Lord, it was a pleasant surprise to awaken from my operation to find my golf clubs in my room. They're not a religious symbol, but it meant a great deal to me that my friend had put them there.

I love golf, and the golf clubs were an incentive for me to get well. I was uplifted by this thoughtful, imaginative act of love.

Thank you for this sign of love, and the many others I have received. Love renews both mind and body. I thank you that you surround me with your love, and I thank you for the loving people in my life. Lord, keep me in your love, for without love, life diminishes and dies. Amen.

GETTING THROUGH THE NIGHT

Lord, I've made it through another day, but I'm not looking forward to the evening. The nights seem so much longer. The evening with its lack of activity brings my fears to the fore, and I'm more conscious of my pain.

Lord, help me to get through the night. Give me the self-control to take things a day, or indeed a night at a time. Give me the rest I need tonight.

Watch over all who are spending a restless night in this hospital. Comfort the troubled, bless the dying.

" 'Stay with us, for it is nearly evening; the day is almost over.' So he went in to stay with them" (Luke 24:29). Amen.

THE DESERT

Lord, I miss being a part of the everyday world. Since my illness I find myself in a desert of solitude and seclusion. I have been thrown on my own resources in a way I have never been before. My customary diversions have been taken from me, and the "demons" within me are making their presence felt.

I thank you, Lord, that the desert is not just a place of self-knowledge, an encounter with the "demons" within me. I know that the desert is also a place of encounter with you. Indeed, you have said: "I will lead her into the desert and speak tenderly to her" (Hosea 2:14).

Let me hear your word of promise: "I will . . . make the Valley of Achor [trouble] a door of hope" (Hosea 2:15). Amen.

Lost dignity

Lord, I have very little privacy in this hospital. My body is examined, prodded, poked. I am self-conscious about using a bedpan. I am afraid of making a mess.

I know that by themselves these are minor irritants, but it's the loss of dignity that I feel. I feel like a unit on an assembly line.

Lord, you healed a blind man by putting spittle on his eyes. You touched a leper. In simple acts you showed that you did not distance yourself from the sweat, tears, smells, and messiness that are often involved in being sick.

Lord, I thank you that you come to me amid the "indignities" and "messiness" of illness. I thank you that you have simply accepted them. Help me to accept them too. Help me not to dissipate my energies on minor things, but to focus them on getting well. Amen.

GIVE ME OIL IN MY LAMP

Lord, you compared me to waiting virgins with lamps (Matthew 25). You have made me responsible for the oil in my lamp.

You seem to be saying that there are circumstances where I must stand on my own two feet. No one can have faith for me; I either have it or I don't. I must tend my own faith and life's energies as I would the oil in a lamp. I'm sure that's true, Lord.

Since my illness, I know that no others can put themselves entirely in my shoes. This is my illness and no one else's. Help me to find ways to replenish the oil in my lamp. Maybe I need to pray and reflect more on your word. Perhaps a meaningful task would help, or a friend.

Give me oil in my lamp, keep me burning. Amen.

I WANT TO GET WELL

Lord, it would be easy to see myself as merely a victim in this illness. A victim is helpless. A victim is one who has lost all confidence in self-help, who has become passive in outlook.

Lord, you seemed to recognize that people had a part to play in their own healing. You asked blind Bartimaeus what he wanted. "I want to see," he replied. You wanted to see in him some desire or expectation to get well, that you could help, and you rewarded that expectation with the words: "Go . . . your faith has healed you."

Help me, Lord, to feel more in control, and less like a victim. I come to you saying: "I want to be well." Let your answer be to me: "Go . . . your faith has healed you" (Mark 10:52). Amen.

COUNTERFORCES

Lord, my minister came to see me today. I'm grateful for that visit. I found myself expressing the fears I had about my treatment. I talked about my concerns about the future and my family. I grew more confident as I talked. My fears lost their crippling, debilitating hold on me.

I felt counterforces rising up within me. It is as if a barrier had been removed, and positive forces of trust, hope, courage, and perseverance were released.

Thank you, Lord, for that visit. Thank you that I could express my fears. Thank you for the new attitudes my minister was instrumental in unleashing. Thank you for your work in and through this person. Amen.

PERSEVERANCE

My illness is such that I will need the gift of perseverance. Help me to persevere, Lord, and not lose heart. I'm strengthened by the fact that you blessed and rewarded people who persevered.

I identify strongly with the widow in Luke 18 who kept demanding justice from a judge and was eventually granted her request. I am heartened by the unrelenting persistence of the Canaanite woman in Matthew 15 who refused to be sent away until you had responded to her need.

Lord, you urged perseverance in faith and prayer. Strengthen me through your Holy Spirit so that I may continue to persevere, and grant me some signs along the way that my perseverance is bearing fruit. Amen.

GOD'S WILL

Lord, I'm sure that your will is not an impersonal and unalterable fate that I simply have to submit to. I'm sure, too, that your will is more than merely a reference to your commandments. Your will is something that I must seek prayerfully. You want me to find it, since to find it and do it is your path to healing and victory for me.

The cross shows that your will is to save and help all peoples. Enable me, then, to discern your saving will for me at this time, and help me overcome the resistance and obstacles I may encounter in following it.

Lord, I pray earnestly the petition you yourself taught us to pray: "Your will be done," knowing that your will is to save, help, and heal. Amen.

Remember

Lord, I have brought a great deal of unnecessary hardship into my life because I did not remember certain things when I needed to remember them. My life was not focused on you. I forget so easily, particularly when I am distracted by illness and uncertainty as I am now.

Help me to remember your words: "Unless a kernel of wheat falls to the ground and dies, it remains only a single seed. But if it dies, it produces many seeds" (John 12:24). These are words full of promise and your resurrection power.

I thank you, too, for your meal of remembrance. "Do this in remembrance of me," you said.

Help me to live remembering your presence and activity in my life. Help me to live a focused life that looks to you and your word for help and healing. Amen.

CHANGE FOR THE BETTER

My illness has been a shock to me, Lord. It has been a powerful reminder to me that my stay on earth is only temporary.

I feel I have changed. My work no longer has the same significance for me. I feel differently about many of my friends. My dreams, hopes, and wishes have changed. I feel I am less attached to many things, and I am trusting you more.

This is a change for the better, Lord. Thank you for this change in me and my growing inner freedom. Thank you that in fact in this freedom I "possess" the world and my life more as it should be possessed. Thank you, Lord, that I am possessed by you more fully. Amen.

Loss and Compensation

Lord, this illness has left me with a sense of loss. My capacity for work and certain enjoyments has been diminished. I know I am not the same person I was before, and I have found this realization painful.

Thank you, Lord, that you have shown me signs of hope. I see how a blind person compensates for the loss of sight with a keener sense of touch and hearing. I heard a deaf percussionist perform by feeling the vibrations of the sounds through the soles of her feet.

Lord, you compensate us for our losses. You say in your word: "We do not lose heart. Though outwardly we are wasting away, yet inwardly we are being renewed day by day" (2 Corinthians 4:16). I thank you, Lord, that you lead me, not to a diminished life but always to the more abundant life. Amen.

THE MIND

Lord, scientists marvel at the extraordinary power of the mind to heal the body. But it's not just the mind as such that has healing power; it's what is in my mind that counts.

So the apostle Paul writes: "Whatever is true, whatever is noble, whatever is right, whatever is pure, whatever is lovely . . . think about such things" (Philippians 4:8). At the same time, the apostle knew that what is true, pure, and lovely flows from you and your presence in our lives.

Lord, I marvel at the power of the mind to heal. Be in my mind; shape my understanding and outlook. Do your healing work in my mind and through it in my body. Amen.

A FIGHTING SPIRIT

"It's God's will," someone said. "You will have to accept it." Lord, I'm sure that not everything that happens to me requires my humble submission and acceptance. As I see it, acceptance of my illness is only desirable when nothing more can be done.

Help me, Lord, to fight this illness. Give me a buoyant, determined spirit. Help me not to fall into the trap of accepting something I need not and should not accept.

I know too, Lord, that the best way to fight my illness is not to tense myself up inwardly for some supposed conflict, but paradoxically to rest. Help me to fight by resting in you, knowing that you will fight in me and for me: "When my enemies and my foes attack me, they will stumble and fall" (Psalm 27:2). Amen.

A DARK MYSTERY

Lord, since my illness you have become a dark mystery to me. St. John of the Cross described you as the "Cloud of Unknowing," against which he continually had to beat with his prayers.

That's how I feel now. There's nothing I can do but sit in this darkness and wait and pray.

That's what I'm going to do, Lord, until I sense your loving presence in the cloud; until the stirrings of your goodness rise up within me again. Lord, I'm trusting that what St. Paul says is true when he reassures me that "Suffering produces perseverance; perseverance, character; and character, hope. And hope does not disappoint us" (Romans 5:3-5). Amen.

ON THE RIGHT TRACK

Lord, I know that you are always seeking loving communion with me. You have a path, a way for me. You are always calling me onto that path.

Instead of hearing your call, I so often continue to tread the path of self-pity, resentment, and anxiety. Since my illness, this path has had a peculiar hold on me. I want to leave that path, Lord.

Jesus, you said that you are the path. Grant me your Holy Spirit to guide and lead me on your path. Help me know better your love and compassion, and enable me to trust your power and will to help and heal. Give me confidence that I am on the right track, and help me follow it. Amen.

A NEW EXPERIENCE

Lord, illness is a totally new experience for me. It's taking me time to absorb what it means and how to accommodate it. I experience life now in the midst of uncertainty, anxiety, and sometimes pain. It has also meant that I experience you in the midst of uncertainty, pain, and fear, and that's something new to me too.

I notice how your pain and fear, Lord Jesus, help me overcome my own. I praise you for your love that took you the way of the cross.

Lord, I'm still sick, but your love is making me more whole. I know that in time this wholeness will also aid the healing of my body. Is that what my illness means? Is this what I need to understand and accommodate? Amen.

WRESTLING

Lord, Jacob wrestled with you, determined not to let you go unless you blessed him. Grant me faith and bless me, so that I can wrestle constructively with this illness.

I need your blessing, Lord, because your blessing is not just a promise of better things in the future. Your blessing is to know and possess something of your abundant life now, and you know how much I am in need of that.

I know that only your blessing can impart that abundant life and allow me to be like St. Paul: "sorrowful, yet always rejoicing; poor, yet making many rich; having nothing, and yet possessing everything" (2 Corinthians 6:10).

Bless me as I wrestle with this illness, Lord. "I will not let you go unless you bless me" (Genesis 32:26). Amen.

CONFIDENCE

Lord, help me retain a confident, trusting disposition, even though I am sick. Help me not lapse into complaining and self-pity.

I'm sure "positive self-talk" is helpful here, because it's so easy to give myself messages that I can't cope, and that it's all too hard. I'm sure too, Lord, that "positive God-talk" is even more important.

I thank you that I can recall your many promises to me. I thank you that I can call upon you in prayer. I thank you for the security your coming in your word gives me—a firm foundation from which I can observe the ebb and flow of events around me. I thank you for the confident trust your word brings. Help me sink roots in it. Amen.

OUT OF THE COLD

Lord, I do all I can to escape the cold. Severe cold can be distressing, even life-threatening.

Lord, I do all I can to avoid physical cold, but often seem powerless to overcome inner cold. Illness can be inwardly chilling. It isolates me, creates a barrier to fellowship with others. It brings feelings of inadequacy, because I am not like others at this particular time. The uncertainty of illness and what lies ahead makes me selfish, and even bitter.

Thank you for your word, Lord, with its warmth and light. I thank you for your Spirit, who brings to me the fire of your love. I thank you for people who have exuded warmth and caring to me in my sickness. I thank you, Lord, for continually bringing me in from the cold, into your light and warmth. Amen.

BEFORE SURGERY

Lord, you know all my needs at this time. You know what my body needs, and you know my inner needs better than I know them myself.

I know, Lord, you healed and comforted the sick and distressed. Grant that my body may be healed through this operation I am about to face, and comfort me with your loving presence.

Enable me continually to hand all my cares about myself and my loved ones to you.

Watch over me as I lose consciousness, and let me awake full of resolve to do all I can to return to health again. Amen.

A COMPASSION THAT RAISES UP

Lord, when you were in Nain you observed a sad little procession winding its way to the cemetery. Of all the people in the procession, it was the grieving mother who caught your attention. You simply could not go past this distressed person. You raised her dead son.

I see in this act a great demonstration of your power over sickness and death. I naturally focus on the youth you raised to life, but you focused on the distress and grief of this mother. She was at the center of your thoughts.

Lord, I praise you for your compassion, a compassion that I know extends also to me. Your compassion inspires me and raises me up in confident hope and trust to deal with my illness and face the future boldly. Amen.

Faith and healing

Lord, you always linked faith with answer to prayer. You said: "I tell you, whatever you ask for in prayer, believe that you have received it, and it will be yours" (Mark 11:24).

Lord, I have asked to be well, but no miracle has occurred. I readily admit that my faith is weak and vacillating. But I find comfort in the fact that your disciples also struggled with faith. The Emmaus disciples were in the depths of despair, and then at the end of their walk had hearts burning with faith— only later to have these hearts filled with fear yet again.

Lord, faith seems more like a mountain path. No sooner do I reach the top, than I discover that there is a valley below to be traversed. Still, through it all I know you are strengthening my faith. Continue to strengthen it, Lord, and through it remove the obstacles to the work of your healing in me. Amen.

PRAYER OF A PERSON WITH AIDS

Lord, at times I feel like the lepers of Jesus' day. Although I receive care, I feel shut out and alone. I sense the reluctance of some to be involved with me. They'd rather I had some other disease, or that I would just go away.

Lord, I have to bear my fears alone. I find that my disease does not so much attract the compassion of people as it attracts their prejudices. This fills me with anger at times.

I am helped in the knowledge that you touched lepers. You sought to overcome their isolation and stigma. You died a lonely death.

Risen Lord, touch me now with your loving presence. Dispel this anger and despair. I thank you that you are my companion and friend. Amen.

O Lᴏʀᴅ my God, I called to you for help
   and you healed me.
O Lᴏʀᴅ, you brought me up from the
      grave;
   you spared me from going down-into
      the pit.
Sing to the Lᴏʀᴅ, you saints of his;
   praise his holy name.
For his anger lasts only a moment,
   but his favor lasts a lifetime;
weeping may remain for a night,
   but rejoicing comes in the morning.
                              Psalm 30:2-5
Amen.